Who Was
Charlie Chaplin?

Who Was
Charlie Chaplin?

by Patricia Brennan Demuth

illustrated by Gregory Copeland

Grosset & Dunlap
An Imprint of Penguin Random House

For my sisters, Mary, Rite, and Tess—
with laughter and love—PBD

For my dad—GC

J-B
CHAPLIN
450-2012

GROSSET & DUNLAP
Penguin Young Readers Group
An Imprint of Penguin Random House LLC

Text copyright © 2016 by Patricia Brennan. Illustrations copyright © 2016 by Penguin Random House LLC. All rights reserved. Published by Grosset & Dunlap, an imprint of Penguin Random House LLC, 345 Hudson Street, New York, New York 10014. Who HQ™ and all related logos are trademarks owned by Penguin Random House LLC. GROSSET & DUNLAP is a trademark of Penguin Random House LLC. Printed in the USA.

Library of Congress Cataloging-in-Publication Data is available.

ISBN 9780448490168 (paperback)   10 9 8 7 6 5 4 3 2 1
ISBN 9780399542411 (library binding)   10 9 8 7 6 5 4 3 2 1

Contents

Who Was Charlie Chaplin?

In the early 1900s, movie theaters across America rocked with laughter. It was all because of a funny little guy on the big screen. His pants and shoes were too large. His hat and coat were too small. He walked in an oddball way with both feet turned outward. And when his eyes grew big and he twitched his little mustache, the audience couldn't wait to see what trouble he would get into next. The screen character was called the Little Tramp.

Charlie Chaplin was the actor behind the mustache. He invented the Little Tramp. Charlie also wrote, starred, and directed his own movies. The Little Tramp was always broke and out of work. But Charlie himself was the highest-paid actor in the world—and the most famous. He managed all that without saying a word on-screen.

This was the age of silent films. No sound came from the screen. Inventors hadn't yet found a way to record sound for films. Instead, actors used gestures and facial expressions to act out the story, as in a game of charades. There was none better at this than Charlie Chaplin.

Although his "reel life" was filled with humor, Charlie's real life was not. His poor London childhood had been heartbreaking. His father deserted the family. And his mother couldn't care for her children properly because of mental breakdowns. Yet history remembers Charlie with a smile. He was a pioneer in film who tickled America's funny bone.

CHAPTER 1
Poverty

America was where Charlie became famous. But England was his first home. Charles Spencer Chaplin was born in London on April 16, 1889. His half brother, Sydney, was four years older.

It's not surprising that Charlie grew up to be an actor: Both of his parents were entertainers.

They performed in English music halls—theaters that staged shows featuring many song and dance acts as well as comedy routines. His father was a successful actor and songwriter. His mother was a singer.

Charles Chaplin Sr. was easygoing and charming, but he had a bad drinking problem. No one could rely on him for long. When Charlie was just one, his father packed up his songs and left.

Charlie's mother, Hannah, did the best she could on her own. She was small and delicate, with hair so long she could sit on it. Though she faced life with spirit, jobs came and went, and money was often tight.

Music Halls

Music halls hosted live shows with a dazzling variety of acts. Acrobats flew through the air. Ventriloquists spoke through dummies. Singers and dancers performed. There

were high-wire walkers, animal trainers, and plate spinners. Most popular of all were the comedy acts.

In the United States, music halls were known as *vaudeville* (VAUD-vill) theaters. The biggest days for vaudeville were the early 1900s. Once movies became popular, music halls and vaudeville gradually faded into history.

Still, the little household was happy for a while. Hannah taught Charlie to dance almost as soon as he could stand. To entertain her sons, Hannah pulled costumes and wigs from her trunk and acted out plays that she knew by heart.

One night, Hannah's singing career came to a sudden end. Her voice cracked in the middle of a song. The crowd hissed and booed Hannah off the stage. The frantic manager pushed little Charlie onstage in her place! Charlie was just five, but he had been watching from backstage for years. He knew all the numbers by heart.

As the small boy began to sing and dance, the crowd grew silent. Soon they were laughing and cheering. Then they threw pennies onto the stage. Charlie stopped in the middle of the song to scoot around and pick up the money. The crowd laughed even harder.

Charlie was a hit. However, Hannah's career was over. She never sang again. "That night was my first appearance on the stage," Charlie later wrote, "and Mother's last."

The family began sinking deeper and deeper into poverty. Hannah earned a little money sewing, but not enough to pay the bills. She tore up her old costumes to make clothes for her sons. Often short of rent money, the Chaplins were forced to move again and again. They started out in a three-room apartment. Then they moved into two rooms. Finally, they crowded into one room behind a smelly pickle factory.

In time Hannah was too weak and ill to go on. She led her sons to the workhouse. That was where poor people ended up in London when there was no place else to go.

The little family was split apart. Hannah was put in an infirmary, a place for people too sick to earn their keep in the workhouse. Charlie and Sydney were taken to a school for homeless children, called Hanwell. Charlie clung tightly to his older brother, but Sydney had to stay in a ward with older boys. Charlie later said that his childhood ended right then. He was seven.

Hanwell School for Orphans

The English Workhouse

During Charlie's childhood, poor people who couldn't pay their bills were sent to the workhouse. There they worked for their rooms and meals, if they were able. Families were split up and only met briefly, once a day. Everyone wore uniforms, slept in long dorms, and ate on benches in large dining halls. No one wanted to end up in the workhouse. Yet it probably saved many from starving on the streets.

Teachers at Hanwell were strict. They used a cane to punish children. One time Charlie was caned for not telling on some boys who had pulled a prank. His knuckles were rapped because he wrote left-handed. When his head was shaved because of ringworm, Charlie broke down and wept.

Daydreaming was Charlie's great escape. In his autobiography, Charlie recalled "creeping off by myself at the poorhouse and pretending I was a very rich and grand person."

More than anything, the little boy wanted to escape poverty. In time, acting would become Charlie's ticket out of the slums. And he was soon to get his first job.

CHAPTER 2
Onstage

In the fall of 1898, the law caught up with Charlie's father and made him take in his sons. You would think Charlie would prefer anything to the workhouse. But he said that was "a stick of candy" compared to two months with his father. Charles Sr. lived with a woman who didn't want Charlie and Sydney around. When their father was away, she ordered the boys out of the house. Sometimes the brothers had to huddle in doorways and sleep in alleys.

At last Hannah got out of the hospital and rescued them. The boys never again lived with their father. Just three years later, Charles Sr. would die from alcohol abuse at age thirty-eight.

Charlie now attended school off and on— mostly off. 1898 became his last full-time year at school. He was only nine.

When he played hooky, Charlie tried to earn a few pennies. One way was clog dancing on the street for a musician with a barrel organ. Passersby tossed coins into a hat.

One afternoon, a well-dressed gentleman watched his dancing. The man, William Jackson, managed a group of boys who clog danced in music halls around London. They were called the Eight Lancashire Lads. Right now, Jackson had only seven lads. In Charlie, he found his eighth. When Hannah gave her permission, Charlie began his first real job.

Charlie thought he'd hit the jackpot! Four of the Lancashire Lads were children of Mr. and Mrs. Jackson. But the kindly couple treated all the dancers as family. Charlie had a free room. Food was free, too. And he earned about a dollar a week, which he sent home to his mother.

The Lads trained hard. Cloggers hold their arms still at their sides while their feet fly to the beat of the music.

On show nights, the dancers sped from one music hall to the next in horse-drawn carts.

Charlie loved to watch the other acts, especially the
clowns and comedians. "Every move they made
registered on my young brain like a photograph,"
he said. "I used to try it all when I got home."
Charlie also learned to juggle and do acrobatic
stunts.

After more than two years with the Lads, Charlie's mother brought him home. She thought her son looked worn out. But Charlie didn't stop working. He often took odd jobs. He worked at a barbershop, a doctor's office, and a stationery store. He became a printer's helper and a glassblower's assistant. Years later, many of these work settings appeared in Charlie's movies.

Still, there was never enough money. Charlie and his mother lived in a tiny top-floor room. (Sydney was away at sea.) Hannah's small iron bed stood in one corner. Charlie slept in an armchair that unfolded into a bed.

In 1903, Charlie grew alarmed at his mother's state of mind. Hannah seemed to be losing her grip on reality. For hours Hannah gazed out the window without stirring. Dirty dishes piled up. Sometimes she heard imaginary voices.

One day, Hannah went door-to-door handing out pieces of wrapped coal as gifts. Charlie knew his mother needed the kind of care he was not able to give. So he walked her to the nearest clinic, a mile away. From there, doctors sent Hannah to a mental hospital. Except for short periods, she would remain in different hospitals for the next seventeen years.

Charlie walked home alone to the empty apartment. The cupboards were bare except for tea. He prowled the streets, looking for food and work. Then word came that his big brother's ship was coming in. "If Sydney had not returned to London, I might have become a thief in the London streets," Charlie said.

Sydney was shocked to see Charlie's rags and long, dirty hair. He quickly got him a hot bath, a haircut, and a new suit. Then he laid out his plan: Sydney was going to start acting. Charlie decided to try it, too.

Hannah Chaplin (1865–1928)

Hannah Chaplin never fully recovered her mental health after her breakdown in 1903. She had to remain under nursing care for the rest of her life, even after her sons got her a cottage by the sea in  California in 1921. She died there in 1928 at age sixty-three.

Charlie always preferred to remember his mother in better times. "It seems to me that my mother was the most splendid woman I ever knew," he told a reporter. "I can remember how charming and well-mannered she was."

The Chaplin brothers soon landed theater jobs. Charlie played a young boy in *Sherlock Holmes*. Getting the job thrilled him—until he got the script. With so little schooling, he couldn't read it! So Sydney read aloud the lines until, in three days, Charlie knew them by heart.

For the rest of his life, Charlie could recite the play, word for word.

Sherlock Holmes became a smash hit. Charlie was in the play for over two years. By the end, he was determined to make acting his life.

He just didn't know it would be in comedy.

CHAPTER 3
Slapstick Comedy

Fred Karno

In 1908, Charlie stood in the office of Fred Karno, asking for a job. The showman was a beefy guy who smoked a big cigar. He managed a famous group of slapstick comedians. Slapstick comedy abounds with punches, falls, sprawls, bumps, and pies in the face.

Charlie's brother, Sydney, already worked for Karno. But Karno didn't think Charlie would fit in at all. Charlie stood only five feet four inches tall. His hands and feet were small. "I thought he looked much too shy," said Karno.

"Seventeen's very young," Karno told Charlie, "and you look even younger."

Charlie shrugged and said that wasn't a big problem, just "a question of make-up."

Karno agreed to try out the teenager for two weeks.

For his opening night, Charlie entered the stage with his back to the audience. They saw a well-to-do gentleman wearing a top hat and fancy cape. Then Charlie turned around.

He had painted his nose bright red!

There was a ripple of laughter. So Charlie started to clown. He veered across the stage, tripping over a dumbbell. When he caught his cane on an upright punching bag, it slapped him in the face. Charlie staggered and swung back, landing his cane on the side of his head. The audience roared.

By the end of the week, the crowd clapped as soon as Charlie came onstage. Karno knew he had a winner. He signed Charlie on the spot.

Karno's Speechless Comedians performed in music halls all over England and Europe. Charlie performed in three shows a night, seven days a week.

Rehearsals filled the days. Onstage, the players acted clumsy or drunk, but their gags actually required split-second timing, like the steps of a difficult dance. Why? Because slapstick often involves chain reactions. One player might throw a punch, the second guy ducks, and a third man takes the blow. No one ever got hurt, though. Offstage someone clapped sharply at each fake punch.

Charlie quickly became an expert at taking wild tumbles. He made the hardest stunts look easy. Soon Karno raised Charlie from bit parts to starring roles. In the fall of 1910, he offered Charlie a chance to go to America on a tour.

The Karno troupe landed in New York City
in late September. That night, Charlie walked
along Broadway. Theater lights twinkled all
around. Skyscrapers loomed above his head.
Charlie thought America offered opportunity

and adventure. *This is where I belong!* he told himself. Charlie made up his mind right then and there to stay.

America loved Charlie right back. Rave reviews poured in for his act: Chaplin is the "biggest laugh-maker." "He is a "born comedian." His entrance alone "sets the house in a roar."

Offstage, however, Charlie was quiet and reserved. Some of the guys thought Charlie was unfriendly, said his roommate Stan Laurel. (Laurel later became famous in the Laurel and Hardy comedy act.) "He wasn't, he wasn't at all. . . . He is a very, very shy man."

Stan Laurel

During the long cross-country train rides, Charlie buried his nose in a book. His schooling had been cut so short. Now Charlie was determined to educate himself by reading. He also taught himself to play the violin. First Charlie had to reverse the strings. It was the only way he could play left-handed.

One day in 1913, a telegram came for him. By then, Charlie had spent five years with Karno. The telegram invited him to come to California and make movies!

WESTERN UNION
TELEGRAM

RECEIVED AT: NEW YORK CITY NY JUNE 12 1913

CHARLES CHAPLIN

KEYSTONE STUDIOS OF EDENDALE CALIFORNIA REQUESTS THE PLEASURE OF YOUR COMPANY AT OUR FILM COMPANY AS EARLIEST AS POSSIBLE STOP WE WILL PROVIDE ARRANGEMENTS FOR LODGING AS WELL AS ALL EXPENSES STOP PLEASE MEET OUR NEW YORK REPRESENTATIVE FOR CONFIRMATION AT THE WALDORF HOTEL AT FOUR O'CLOCK ON FRIDAY JUNE 20 STOP

It was a big risk. Charlie had always acted onstage, not in front of a camera. And the movie business was still young. The first US movie theater had opened its doors just eight years earlier.

"I hated to leave [Karno]," Charlie said later. "Suppose I didn't make good?"

No worries there, Charlie!

CHAPTER 4
The Big Screen

In December, 1913, Charlie showed up for his first day at Keystone Studios. Only a year old, Keystone was one of several small movie studios that had sprouted up in sunny California. Its most popular movies were about the Keystone Kops, a fumbling group of policemen who dashed around on wild chases. The same group of actors performed in every film.

The Keystone Kops in their patrol car

The studio was five miles outside of Los Angeles. To Charlie, it looked like a big dumpy warehouse. Old farms, wooden shacks, and stores were nearby, along with cactus and sagebrush. The actors at the studio looked like roughnecks. Charlie turned around and went straight back to his hotel!

It took three days before Charlie finally returned to Keystone. A huge platform, two blocks long, stretched the length of the studio.

Three or four different movies were filmed at the same time. The sets stood side by side. One might be a living room, another a prison, and a third a skating rink. Charlie was fascinated.

A roar filled the studio. Carpenters sawed lumber and pounded nails to build new sets. Cameras cranked. Directors shouted orders. The racket didn't matter at all, of course: Movies had no sound.

Movie studios didn't use electric lighting at the time, either. Even though electric lights were widely used by then, none were powerful enough to expose film. Instead, bright California sunshine lit the studio.

Charlie was given a few days to look around to see how movies were made. Some things surprised him. He heard a director shout "cut!" after an actress had only pounded on a door. That was when Charlie learned that movies were made in little pieces. The scenes were filmed out of order and later spliced together in the editing room.

When Charlie was ready to play his first role, there was another surprise: Keystone made movies without a script. Directors started filming with only a loose idea of the story. The actors and directors made up most of the gags on the spot. "In the theater I had been confined to a rigid routine of repeating the same thing night after night," wrote Charlie, "but films were freer. They gave me a sense of adventure."

A couple of days later, Charlie's first movie, *Making a Living* (1914), was done. Movies at that time were called "shorts." They were one reel long, or about fifteen minutes. Keystone often made three movies a week!

Scene from *Making a Living*, Charlie on the left

For Charlie's second movie, the cast was going to drive to a kids' derby-car race in nearby Venice, California. Keystone movies were often filmed "on location" rather than inside a studio. For instance, a movie might be shot at a parade,

Mack Sennett

outdoor concert, horse race, or even a local fire. Real-life scenes were interesting, plus they cost nothing to produce. Mack Sennett was the head of Keystone. Before the cast left for Venice, he told Charlie to put together a costume. He could dress any way he wanted.

Charlie searched through Keystone's large

costume room—an old barn—and took whatever caught his fancy. He later wrote, "I wanted everything a contradiction: the pants baggy, the coat tight, the hat small and the shoes large."

Once dressed, Charlie pulled a huge pair of patched shoes on the wrong feet. Then he pasted on a small black mustache, grabbed a cane, and shambled outdoors.

He didn't know it then, but he was about to make movie history.

Charlie had just invented the famous character that became known as the Little Tramp. *Kid Auto Races at Venice* (1914) was the first movie with the Tramp in it. Two days later, he appeared in *Mabel's Strange Predicament* (1914), and in that movie the Tramp's funny personality came to life. He stumbles over a lady's foot and raises his hat to apologize. Then he staggers over a spittoon and tips his hat to that, too. He gives an elegant twirl to his cane and knocks off his own hat.

As the filming went on, Charlie heard the cameraman start to laugh. Soon others in the Keystone crew left their sets to watch the clowning. "That indeed was a compliment," Charlie recalled later. "I then and there decided I would keep to this costume [and Tramp character], whatever happened."

True to his word, Charlie played the Tramp for the next twenty-two years in about seventy films. He had created one of the most famous characters ever to appear on-screen after just five days in the movies!

CHAPTER 5
Director and Star

The movies had Charlie hooked. He set about learning every part of filmmaking. How was film cut and spliced in the editing room? Where could actors move and still stay within the camera range? At what speeds were the cameras cranked to hurry up or slow down the action? (Silent movies often raced at a pace faster than real life, for comic effect.)

No one worked harder than Charlie. "He wanted to work—and nearly all the time," said Mack Sennett. "We went to work at eight o'clock and he was there at seven. We quit at five . . . but he'd still be around at six."

Unfortunately, Charlie's style sometimes clashed with Keystone's. Their comedies focused on a pell-mell chase. Charlie thought that the best comedy was based on character. He wanted to add funny details to his scenes that played on the Tramp's personality. But directors didn't want to slow down the superfast pace. Some of Charlie's funniest bits ended up on the cutting-room floor.

Charlie began to dream of writing and directing his own movies.

For one picture, actress Mabel Normand was the director. She was a star at the time.

Mabel Normand

During an outdoor shoot, she refused to listen to any of Charlie's ideas. Finally Charlie walked off and sat down on the curb.

Silent Films 1894–1929

Movies were made
on big reels of film.

Cameras were cranked
by hand.

Live music
at the theater
set a mood.

Projectionists
cranked the film.

Title cards
flashed on
the screen.

Dawn.

A
DOG'S LIFE

Written and Produced by
CHARLES CHAPLIN
MCMXVIII

Mack Sennett was furious when he heard about Charlie's sit-down strike. "Do what you're told," he yelled at Charlie. Then he marched off.

Charlie figured he'd be fired. But to his surprise, Sennett met him with a friendly smile the next day. He had just learned from his bosses on the East Coast that Charlie's films were outselling all other Keystone movies! They wanted more pictures with that funny Tramp guy right away.

Sennett had to find a way to make Charlie happy. Charlie suggested that he direct his own movies. That sounded risky to Sennett. Charlie was still new to movies, after all. Then Charlie said he'd put his life savings on the line. Keystone would not lose a cent. That sealed the deal. From then on, Charlie was both director and star of his films.

Charlie loved thinking up gags for the Tramp. He always did the unexpected. Not knowing how to milk a cow, the Tramp might pull its tail. When drenched with a hose, the Tramp twisted his ear and water poured from his mouth. Tripping over his shadow, the Tramp tipped his hat to it.

In between scenes, Charlie entertained the crew by clog dancing or doing headstands. To direct his cast, Charlie acted out all their parts before shooting.

A seat at the movies cost only a nickel or dime at that time. Movies were shown in small theaters called nickelodeons, converted from old stores. Sometimes Charlie slipped into a theater where his film was playing. No one recognized the handsome young man with the deep blue eyes. He looked nothing at all like the funny hobo on film. Charlie didn't watch the screen. His eyes and ears were focused on the audience. When did they chuckle? What made them laugh hard? The audience feedback helped Charlie shape his next film.

Nickelodeons

The first movie theaters were nickelodeons. Working-class people, including millions of immigrants, flocked to them.

Nickelodeons were shabby and poor. No refreshments were served, and viewers sat in wooden chairs. For just a nickel, viewers watched black-and-white shorts lasting ten to fifteen minutes.

Up until then, movie actors had not been named on the screen. Now the public demanded to know who *was* that guy behind the mustache? Big cut-outs of the Tramp started popping up in front of theaters all around America. "Charlie Chaplin. I am here to-day," the signpost read. The Chaplin name became a big draw.

After one year at Keystone, Charlie was ready to move on. A year isn't a very long time. But he had already made thirty-five movies!

CHAPTER 6
Fame

Charlie asked his brother, Sydney, to be his business manager. It proved to be a wise move. Sydney landed Charlie a contract with Essanay Film Studios. They paid about thirty times as much as Keystone had!

Charlie started to turn out about one Tramp comedy a month. Most were two reels long, lasting about a half hour. But hours and hours of filming went into every scene. Charlie did endless retakes. An actor for *The Tramp* (1915) told Stan Laurel about shooting a ladder scene fifty times. "The actors felt that if they did it one more time they'd blow their corks," Laurel reported. But Charlie was a great artist. "He just absolutely refused to do anything but the best."

On the screen, Charlie made everything look easy. Fans came to know and adore his funny style. The Tramp skidded around corners with one foot in the air. He threw a match over his shoulder and kicked it with his heel.

He rolled his hat down the length of his arm and made it spring off his head without touching it. The Tramp did crazy somersaults—forward, backward, and three quarters. Just before mischief started, he arched his eyebrows or twitched his mustache.

Most important, the Tramp stood for the little guy who never gives up. His spirit shines through in the famous ending of *The Tramp*. He has just lost his sweetheart to a tall, handsome man. In a fade-out shot, he trudges along down a long road alone. A bandana on a stick is slung over his shoulder.

Suddenly, the Tramp does a happy little hop and twirls his cane. Life might knock him down, but the Tramp always picks himself up again.

In 1916, Sydney called Charlie to New York to sign a new contract with the Mutual Film Corporation. Charlie took the train there. At a stop in Albuquerque, he heard cheers outside. Word had leaked that Charlie was on the train. Fans had mobbed the station to see him.

A Chaplin craze was sweeping America. Stores sold Tramp dolls, buttons, comic books, hats, and playing cards. Tramp look-alike contests were held. In Europe, Charlie became a superstar very quickly because silent movies didn't have to be translated into another language. In Spain, they cheered for *Carlitos;* in France, *Charlot;* in Italy, *Carlo.*

Charlie's longing for wealth now came true beyond his wildest dreams. His Mutual contract of 1916 paid him $10,000

a week. That made him the highest-paid person in America—maybe even the world. It was an outstanding amount in an age when a quarter could buy a dozen eggs. Just a year later, he signed a contract with First National that made him a millionaire! He'd gone from rags to riches.

Sydney Chaplin

Sydney was an infant when his mother, Hannah, married Charles Chaplin Sr. in 1885. Charles adopted Sydney and gave him his last name, Chaplin. Four years later, Charlie was born.

Sydney himself became a fine actor, after first spending several years as a seaman. He rose to leading actor for Karno, where he helped his little brother get a job. Charlie later returned the favor when he helped Sydney get hired as a Keystone actor. While continuing to act, Sydney also served as Charlie's business manager, pulling in superb money deals.

The brothers were very close all their lives. Sydney, stable and caring, kept careful watch over the younger Charlie. Sydney once wrote him, "Since Mother's illness, all we have in the world is each other."

Sydney spent his last years in Europe, where he died at age eighty.

CHAPTER 7
A New Studio

Charlie had always been careful about money, living in just a two-room apartment. But now he finally started to spend. He bought his first car, a seven-seat Locomobile, and hired a driver who stayed with him for twenty years. He also hired a secretary and butler.

His social life was still quiet. Splashy Hollywood parties didn't appeal to him at all. He neither drank nor smoked. At home, he was a charming host, though.

His best friend was Douglas Fairbanks, the dashing star of the *Robin Hood* movies. The two men were opposites. Douglas was outgoing; Charlie was private. But they shared a sense of adventure, a love of tennis, and a lively sense of humor.

Douglas Fairbanks

Most of Charlie's time was spent working. He wrote, directed, starred in, and edited all his films. He also did his own casting.

In *A Dog's Life* (1917), a stray dog named Scraps becomes the Tramp's pal. Charlie tested—and rejected—several purebred dogs for the part. Then he found a runt named Mutt at the local pound. Delighted, Charlie cast him in the movie and kept him on as a studio mascot.

That year, Charlie began building his own studio. He bought five acres on Sunset Boulevard in the heart of Hollywood. Lemon and peach trees bloomed in the lot. He planted a large garden and put in a swimming pool and tennis court. The dream studio was designed to look like a row of English cottages. Inside were offices, stages, dressing rooms, a place to create the reels—and, of course, a cutting room. In 1918, the studio was finished. Chaplin stepped outside into the wet cement and laid his footprints. They were the Tramp's big boots facing outward.

By this time, the United States was fighting in World War I. Charlie decided to put the Tramp in uniform. The little guy wasn't exactly fit for duty. In *Shoulder Arms* (1918), a stern sergeant orders the Tramp to march in a straight line. But his feet keep springing outward. To prepare for battle, the Tramp takes along emergency supplies: things like a coffeepot, a cheese grater, and an eggbeater!

When the movie was almost done, Charlie feared it wasn't funny enough. He was ready to throw it in the trash can. Then his buddy Douglas Fairbanks saw the footage and laughed till he cried. So did the audience when Charlie went ahead and released the film. *Shoulder Arms* became an instant smash hit. GIs returning from the war cheered when the Tramp delivered his famous back kick to the enemy Kaiser's rear.

Charlie still lived happily and simply in two rooms. Then three days after *Shoulder Arms* opened, the famous bachelor surprised everyone by marrying a young actress named Mildred Harris. Charlie bought the first house he ever owned. Unfortunately, Charlie and Mildred had very little in common. Two years later, the marriage ended.

Charlie with Mildred Harris

In 1919, Charlie joined other Hollywood stars to form a company to fund and distribute their own films. Called United Artists, it remains successful to this day.

As a producer, Charlie could do whatever he pleased. What he wanted was to make longer, more dramatic films.

CHAPTER 8
Blockbusters

Charlie was watching a little boy named Jackie Coogan do a lively dance on a vaudeville stage. The child charmed the audience, just as Charlie had done at that age. A new idea dawned on Charlie: to make a movie about an orphan child. Children had appeared in movies before. But they'd hardly ever held starring roles.

Jackie Coogan

The Kid (1921) was different from Charlie's other films. It was his first full-length movie as a director, lasting an hour. Instead of scenes loosely held together, it followed a storyline. Most important, it mixed comedy and drama. The opening title card read:

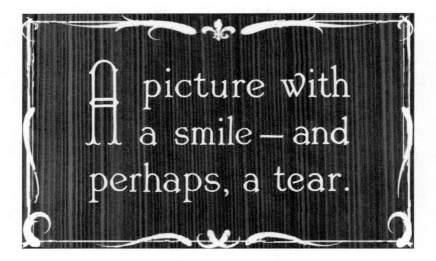

A picture with a smile — and perhaps, a tear.

"It won't work," a famous scriptwriter warned Charlie. "[A movie must be] either slapstick or drama. You cannot mix them." But as usual, Charlie followed his instincts.

The movie shows the Tramp raising a homeless child played by Jackie Coogan. The happy-go-lucky pair survives through their wits.

Although Charlie's temper sometimes flared

with other actors, an easy bond grew between him and his young co-star. In the film's climax, social workers tear Jackie out of the Tramp's arms. For the first time on screen, the Tramp cries. He races across rooftops and leaps onto a truck to rescue Jackie. By then, there wasn't a dry eye in the house.

The Kid was hailed as a masterpiece. Charlie had raised slapstick to art. Soon the film became a worldwide hit. France declared its opening day a national holiday!

History inspired Charlie's next film, set during the Alaskan Gold Rush. In the late 1890s, thousands of prospectors went to Alaska in search of gold. In *The Gold Rush* (1925), Charlie spent a fortune to create sets that looked like Alaska. He brought in ten husky dogs and a live grizzly bear. Tons of salt and flour were trucked in to build a fake snowfield. Cartloads of confetti were brought in for the blizzard scenes.

The opening was shot in the Sierra Nevada Mountains of California. Charlie hired six hundred extras to play gold diggers. In an unforgettable scene, they snake up the lonely mountain in single file. Then a card flashes on screen:

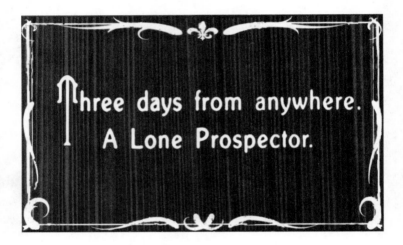

Three days from anywhere. A Lone Prospector.

And there's the Tramp, shuffling along an icy cliff. Of course, his bowler hat is on his head and his cane is in his hand. Before long, the starving Tramp is boiling his boot for Thanksgiving dinner. He serves it up like a special treat, pretending the shoelaces are spaghetti.

Later the Tramp has a dream of hosting a dinner party. He jabs forks into two dinner rolls and pretends they're a pair of shoes dancing. Audiences liked the scene so much that some theaters had to stop the movie and replay it. (Search the key words *Chaplin fork dance* to view it online.)

Fans and critics alike loved *The Gold Rush*. "Chaplin is a genius!" a reviewer wrote in the *New York Herald Tribune*.

While Charlie's film life thrived, his home life suffered. He was going through a second divorce. Though he and his wife, Lita Grey, had two sons together, their marriage was deeply unhappy. Charlie

Lita Grey

stayed so focused on his work that he left little time for his family. Lita was furious over being stuck at home alone—and she let reporters know it. The Chaplins' divorce in 1927 was splashed all over the headlines. Charlie's private life wasn't private at all. Later, the attacks on his character would come back to haunt him.

During the divorce, Charlie was filming *The Circus* (1928). It would become his third masterpiece in a row. The Tramp walks a high wire with monkeys on his back. The treacherous tightrope walk mirrored Charlie's real life.

CHAPTER 9
The Tramp Exits

In the late 1920s, the world of silent movies was turned upside down. Films could now be made with recorded sound! Soon "talkies" became all the rage. Audiences heard the voices of screen stars for the first time. Unfortunately, some had strong accents or thin, squeaky voices. Their careers went bust.

What would Charlie do? He knew the magic of the Little Tramp would be lost as soon as he uttered a word. So Charlie decided to buck the trend. In 1928, he forged ahead on another silent film, *City Lights* (1931). The audience still doesn't hear the Tramp talk. But they hear his hiccups! In a hilarious scene, the Tramp swallows a whistle and hiccups in tweets!

Before now, background music for silent films had been supplied by piano players and organists in local movie houses. Now Charlie could create the music himself. He started writing his own songs! Perhaps he'd inherited the talent from his father. Charlie had never learned to read music, so he hummed the melody and someone else wrote the notes. "Music composer" was added to Charlie's long list of credits.

Movie Theaters

Movie theaters became fancy palaces in the 1920s. The cheap nickelodeons gave way to theaters with marble columns, lavish woodwork, and carpets. Some cost millions to build. By the 1930s, theaters sold refreshments. The smell of popcorn became tied to the movies.

Grauman's Chinese Theatre in Los Angeles

Inside of Fox Theater in Detroit

The biggest changes came when "talkies" arrived. The piano players and organists of the silent-movie era lost their jobs. Huge speakers and new sound equipment were installed in place of them.

City Lights opened in 1931. Would moviegoers still buy tickets for a silent picture? For Charlie, yes! The film became another blockbuster.

It had taken Charlie three years to make *City Lights*. Now it was time for a break—a good long one. Charlie left Hollywood for sixteen months and sailed for Europe and Asia. During the trip, he met with great men like Winston Churchill, Mahatma Gandhi, H. G. Wells, and George Bernard Shaw. He also made a much more private stop.

One day in London, he slipped away by himself and went to Hanwell. The old brick school looked the same as when he'd gone there at seven years old. Charlie stepped inside for a surprise visit. Four hundred boys in the dining room went wild when they recognized him. Charlie went to tip his hat and it sprang off his head like magic. He turned out his feet and did his famous Tramp walk. The boys cheered and screamed. Charlie was one of their own. He proved that humble roots didn't have to hold anyone back.

That night in his hotel room, Charlie wept. Memories of his childhood flooded back. He told the writer Thomas Burke that the visit "had been the greatest emotional experience of his life."

When Charlie returned from his trip, the Great Depression was gripping the country. Millions lost their employment or worked at dead-end jobs for low wages. Charlie felt a deep sympathy for them. He decided to make a comedy with a message. Once again, he dared to do a silent movie. But it would be his last.

Modern Times (1936) shows the Tramp working on a factory assembly line. As a young lad in London, Charlie had worked for a printer. An enormous printing press loomed inside the plant. It scared Charlie to watch the big machine grind and roll. "I thought it was going to devour me," he said. In *Modern Times,* Charlie plays this memory for laughs. The cogs of a monster machine capture the Tramp and the gears chew him.

The hilarious scene also had a serious message. Chaplin worried that factory workers were sometimes treated like parts of a machine, not people.

In the final scene of the movie, the Tramp and his sweetheart have lost everything. But the Tramp cheers her up and tries to get her to smile. Then the pair walks into the distance, hand in hand.

With that, the Little Tramp disappeared from film.

Charlie's Hit Song

Charlie composed a deeply moving melody for the theme song of *Modern Times*. Years later, lyrics were added by John Turner and Geoffrey Parsons. It became a hit song called "Smile." The words capture the Little Tramp's positive, winning spirit:

"Smile though your heart is aching.

Smile even though it's breaking."

Many great singers have recorded "Smile," including Nat King Cole, Michael Jackson, and Barbra Streisand.

CHAPTER 10
Exile

World War II broke out in 1939 when the German dictator Adolf Hitler began his invasion of Poland. Hitler and Charlie had been born just four days apart. The two men even looked somewhat alike. Some

Adolf Hitler

say Hitler chose his stubby mustache because he wanted to be popular, like the Little Tramp. Hitler, however, made it known that he hated Chaplin. He thought Chaplin was Jewish, and Hitler hated all Jews. "I don't have the honor," Charlie stated.

In 1939, Charlie started a film to ridicule the awful tyrant. *The Great Dictator* (1940) became his first talking picture. Charlie played two parts. One was Adenoid Hynkel, a dictator like Hitler. His second role was that of a quiet and dignified Jewish barber.

Charlie showed what Hitler was really like— a ranting, raving, power-hungry maniac. In one famous scene, the dictator dances with a balloon globe. He leaps and romps in a joyful ballet. The globe blows up in his face.

The Great Dictator was a great success—except in Germany, of course. Hitler wouldn't let it be shown. A critic for the *New York Herald Tribune* wrote that the movie was "a savage comic commentary on a world gone mad." Charlie had started the film just one week after the war in Europe began. He said later that he would not have made it if he'd known the horrors of the war that were to come.

Despite the film's success, the 1940s were very hard years for Charlie. He had his first box-office flop. It was a murder mystery named *Monsieur Verdoux* (1947). But much worse, calls came for him to be deported—thrown out of the United States. People suspected him of being a communist.

After World War II ended, there was great tension between the United States and the Soviet Union. They were both superpowers—the only nations capable of dropping a nuclear bomb.

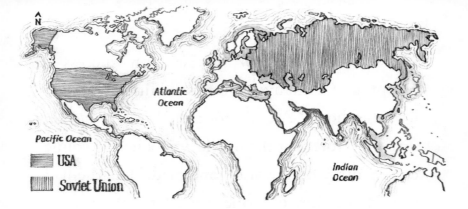

USA

Soviet Union

Although there were no actual battles, the period became known as the Cold War. The Soviet Union was a communist nation. There was only one political party, and people had no freedom under their leaders.

In the United States, panic spread that communists were working in secret within the country to gain power. The US government held hearings of anyone suspected of "un-American activities." (That meant being a communist.) The hearings became a witch hunt. People lost their jobs and found it impossible to get other work. People in the Hollywood film industry were often victims.

But why was Charlie Chaplin a target? For one thing, many thought his political views were too radical. Also, he'd never become a US citizen. When asked why, he answered, "I am a citizen of the world." Charlie had been through three divorces by this time. Each one was dragged through the press. This damaged Charlie's image, too.

Charlie stated firmly that he was not a communist. Although the FBI put together a file of over two thousand pages on Chaplin, nothing was found against him.

In the middle of all this turmoil, Charlie fell in love with Oona O'Neill. The daughter of the famous playwright Eugene O'Neill, she was an intelligent, beautiful woman. And she adored Charlie. They married in June 1943. After three failed marriages, Charlie had finally found long and lasting love. In time, they had eight children.

Oona O'Neill with her father, Eugene O'Neill

In 1952, Charlie sailed for Europe with Oona and their children. They were going to London for the opening of Charlie's third talkie, *Limelight* (1952). (Most American theater owners banned the film.)

After two days at sea, Charlie got word from the US government that he couldn't reenter the country until he had proved himself a loyal citizen. Charlie was angry. His adopted country had turned on him. He decided to leave the United States for good.

The Chaplins roamed Europe awhile, staying in luxury hotels. Then, in 1952, Charlie and Oona bought a beautiful estate in Switzerland. There were sweeping views of the Swiss Alps and sparkling Lake Geneva. Charlie happily spent his last twenty-five years there. The family lived in grand style. A large staff of servants cared for the nineteen-room mansion, built in the 1700s.

Groundskeepers and gardeners tended the thirty-five acre estate.

In Switzerland, Charlie kept busy. He wrote original music for many of his silent movies. That made him the only moviemaker ever to write, act, direct, cast, produce, and compose music for his own films. He also made his last two films, *A King in New York* (1957) and *A Countess from Hong Kong* (1967). Neither one was as popular as his earlier films.

At this late stage in life, Charlie's family life was happier than before. His youngest son was born when Charlie was seventy-three. His grown sons, Charles Jr. and Sydney, also came for visits. Charlie loved sharing his old movies with his kids in the mansion's large viewing room. No one laughed harder than Charlie.

CHAPTER 11
Final Bow

On walks in the Swiss hills, Charlie thought back on his long and full life. In 1964, he put it all down on paper: from painful days at the workhouse to the glory days of the Chaplin craze. The once-wordless  star wrote five hundred pages. *My Autobiography* was translated into many languages and became a best seller around the world.

Now Charlie's curly hair was stark white. He kept fit by swimming and playing tennis. He played soccer on the front lawn with his kids. Finally, in his seventies, his graceful body began to break down. A cane, his old famous prop, now helped him walk.

By this time, feelings toward Charlie in the United States had softened. The old fear of suspected communists had faded. Film historians were praising Charlie's pioneering role in movies. His comedies were timeless, they realized. "Who was the greatest actor in movie history?" a 1995 survey asked film critics. They voted Charlie Chaplin number one.

In 1972, he was given a special Academy Award. It was for his part in "making motion pictures the art form of the century."

To receive his special Oscar, Charlie flew to America. It was the first time he'd been in the United States in twenty years. His first stop was New York City, for a screening of *The Kid*.

Then it was on to Hollywood. When he saw Jackie Coogan, his young sidekick from *The Kid*, Charlie burst into tears. The memory of the good old days in silent film flooded back.

Charlie felt nervous about how the audience at the Oscars would respond to him now. But his fears soon fled. When Charlie came onstage, the audience stood and clapped for twelve minutes. "Oh, you're wonderful, sweet people," he told the

audience, tears sliding down his face.

In 1975, Queen Elizabeth II knighted England's native son. The little street waif was now Sir Charlie Chaplin.

Two years later, on Christmas Day, Chaplin died at home in Switzerland, surrounded by his beloved Oona and children. It was the final scene in a remarkable life. He was eighty-eight.

The year 2016 marked the one hundredth anniversary of Charlie's amazing rise to stardom. To honor the anniversary, a Chaplin museum opened in Charlie and Oona's Swiss mansion.

Praise for Charlie has come from all corners. But Charlie himself once said, "I am just a little nickel comedian trying to make people laugh."

Timeline of Charlie Chaplin's Life

1889	Charles Spencer Chaplin is born in London on April 16
1896	Sent to the Hanwell School for Orphans and Destitute Children
1901	His father, Charles Chaplin Sr., dies of alcohol abuse at thirty-eight
1903	Performs in *Sherlock Holmes*
1908	Showman Fred Karno hires Charlie for his pantomime comedy act
1913	Signs with Keystone Studios
1914	Invents the Little Tramp character
1915	Releases *The Tramp* for Essanay Film Manufacturing Company
1918	*Shoulder Arms* becomes a smash hit
1921	*The Kid,* his first feature film, released to rave reviews
1924	Shooting on *The Gold Rush* (1925) begins
1931	World premiere of *City Lights*
1936	*Modern Times*, set in a factory, opens
1940	*The Great Dictator,* a WWII satire, is released
1943	Marries Oona O'Neill; they will have eight children
1952	His US visa is revoked
	Moves his family to Switzerland
1972	Receives a special Academy Award
1975	Queen Elizabeth II knights Charlie
1977	Dies at home on Christmas Day, at age eighty-eight

Timeline of the World

1900	—	Escape artist Harry Houdini performs for first time in London music halls
1911	—	Several film studios open in Hollywood, California
1913	—	Henry Ford installs the first moving assembly line for mass production of Ford cars
1917	—	The United States enters World War I (1914–1918)
1927	—	*The Jazz Singer* launches the new era of "talking pictures"
1929	—	First Academy Awards ceremony is held in Hollywood
1930	—	England replaces workhouses with aid programs for the poor
1932	—	Walt Disney makes his first color film, a cartoon short called *Flowers and Trees*
1941	—	The US enters World War II (1939–1945) following the Japanese bombing of Pearl Harbor
1950	—	The Korean War begins when communist North Korea invades South Korea
1952	—	Princess Elizabeth is crowned Queen Elizabeth II of England
1954	—	Senator Joseph McCarthy holds public hearings investigating US citizens accused of being communists
1961	—	Disney's *101 Dalmatians* becomes a major hit movie
1963	—	Martin Luther King Jr. gives his famous "I Have a Dream" speech at the March on Washington for Jobs and Freedom
1974	—	Richard Nixon resigns as president of the United States

Bibliography

* Books for young readers

Ackroyd, Peter. *Charlie Chaplin: A Brief Life*. New York: Doubleday, 2014.

Chaplin, Charles. *My Autobiography*. New York: Simon & Schuster, 1964.

Crowther, Bosley. "Charlie Chaplin Dead at 88: Made the Film an Art Form."
New York Times. December 26, 1977.

Douglas, Ann. "The Most Important People of the Century." *The 2010 TIME
100*. June 8, 1998.

*Fleischman, Sid. *Sir Charlie: Chaplin, the Funniest Man in the World*.
New York: Greenwillow Books, 2010.

Lynn, Kenneth S. *Charlie Chaplin and His Times*. New York: Simon &
Schuster, 1997.

McCabe, John. *Charlie Chaplin*. New York: Doubleday, 1978.

Robinson, David. *Chaplin: His Life and Art*. New York: Da Capo Press, 1994.

*Turk, Ruth. *Charlie Chaplin: Genius of the Silent Screen*. Minneapolis,
MN: Lerner Publications, 2000.

Vance, Jeffrey. *Chaplin: Genius of the Cinema*. New York: Abrams, 2003.